Library of Congress Catalog Card Number: 62-9235
Printed in the United States of America

B C D E

LET'S FIND OUT ABOUT

WATER

by

MARTHA and CHARLES SHAPP

Pictures by Richard Mayhew

FRANKLIN WATTS, INC.
575 Lexington Avenue, New York 22

Everybody and everything needs water.
You need water.

Your pets need water.

All animals need water.
Jungle animals need water.

Farm animals need water.

All plants need water.
Plants in the garden need water.

Plants on the farm need water.

Water is needed for washing.
You need water to wash yourself . . .

. . . and to wash your dog.

Water is used to wash everything – from dishes . . .

. . . to streets.

Water is needed to put out fires.

Where does all the water come from?
It comes from the clouds.

Some of the rain sinks into the ground.
Many people get water from under the ground.

Some rain water comes down the mountains in streams.

The streams come together to make lakes.

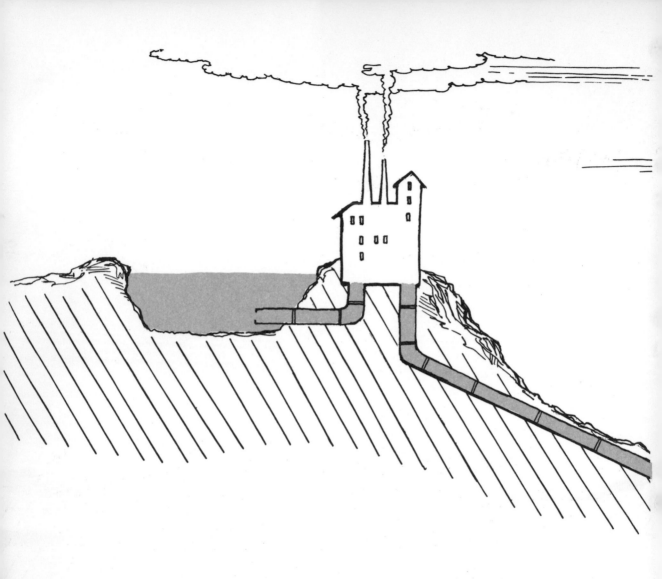

Many people get water from these lakes.
The water is piped from the lakes.

You can have fun with water.

Swimming is fun.

Fishing is fun.

Water can do many things that seem almost like
magic.

It can hold up many things.

A big ship can float in water.

Some things cannot float.
Put a penny into some water.

The penny sinks.

Water can change itself.
When water gets very cold, it becomes ice.

When water gets very hot, it becomes steam.

Water can make things seem to disappear.
Put some sugar into water.
Stir the water.

The sugar seems to have disappeared.
Taste the water.
Is the sugar there?

Water can disappear into the air.
Rain makes the street wet.

The rain stops.
Soon the street is dry.
The water has disappeared into the air.

Mother hangs wet clothes out in the air.

Soon the clothes are dry. The water in the
clothes has disappeared into the air.

39

Water that disappears into the air becomes clouds.

Out of the clouds comes the rain that brings the water.

VOCABULARY LIST (99 words)

a

air

all

almost

and

animals

are

becomes

big

brings

can

cannot

change

clothes

clouds

cold

come(s)

disappear(ed)

dishes

do

does

dog

down

dry

everybody

everything

farm

fires

fishing

float

for

from

fun

garden

get(s)

ground

hangs

has

have

hold

hot

ice

in

into

is

it

itself

jungle

lake(s)

like

magic

make(s)

many

mother

mountains

need(s) (ed)

of

on

out

penny

people

pets

piped

plants

put

rain

seem

ship

sink

some

soon

steam

stir

stops

streams

streets

sugar

swimming

taste

that

the

there

these

things

to

together

under

up

used

very

wash(ing)

water

wet

when

where

with

you

your

yourself